YOU CHOOSE
BOOKS™

WORLD WAR II
SPIES

An Interactive History Adventure

by Michael Burgan

Consultant:
Dennis Showalter, PhD
Professor of History
Colorado College

CAPSTONE PRESS
a capstone imprint

You Choose Books are published by Capstone Press,
1710 Roe Crest Drive, North Mankato, Minnesota 56003
www.capstonepub.com

Library of Congress Cataloging-in-Publication Data
Burgan, Michael.
 World War II spies : an interactive history adventure / by Michael Burgan.
  p. cm. — (You choose books: World War II)
 Summary: "Describes the role spies played during World War II. Readers' choices reveal various
historical details"— Provided by publisher.
 Includes bibliographical references and index.
 ISBN 978-1-4296-9898-6 (library binding)
 ISBN 978-1-62065-722-5 (paperback)
 ISBN 978-1-4765-1814-5 (ebook PDF)
1. World War, 1939-1945—Secret service—Juvenile literature. 2. Espionage—History—20th
century—Juvenile literature. 3. Spies—History—20th century—Juvenile literature. I. Title.
 D810.S7B77 2013
 940.54'85—dc23   2012032724

Editorial Credits
Kristen Mohn, editor; Bobbie Nuytten, designer; Wanda Winch, media researcher;
Jennifer Walker, production specialist

Photo Credits
Alamy: DIZ Muenchen GmbH, Suddeutsche Zeitung Photo, 42, 82; Capstone, 6 (maps); Colby
Family Collection, 68; Corbis, 12; Courtesy of the CGSC, U.S. Army Combined Arms Research
Library, from S.J. Lewis "Jedburgh Team Operations in Support of the 12th Army Group,
August 1944", 9, 85, 97, 103; Courtesy of Ingrid Dockter, dog tag design element; Courtesy of
the Museum of Danish Resistance 1940-1945, Copenhagen, Denmark, 17, 24, 31, 34, 40, 64,
100; Getty Images: Stone/Peter Hince, cover; King's College London: Liddell Hart Centre for
Military Archives, 77, 88; Mary Evans Picture Library: Peter Higginbotham Collection, 59;
National Archives and Records Administration, 94; Newscom: akg-images, 50; The National
Archives of the UK: ref: KV2/458 DN#11251, 55; Shutterstock: Andrey Kuzmin, metal plate
design, Nella, metal texture

Printed in the United States of America in North Mankato, Minnesota.
032018 000015

TABLE OF CONTENTS

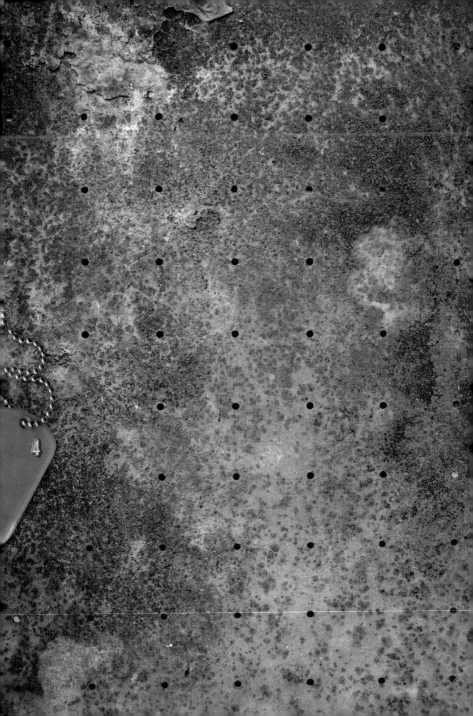

ABOUT YOUR ADVENTURE

The Second World War is brewing in Europe and Asia. Every country involved has secrets they want to keep—and information they want to steal from the enemy. That's where spies come in.

In this book you'll explore how the choices people made meant the difference between life and death. The events you'll experience happened to real people.

Chapter One sets the scene. Then you choose which path to read. Follow the directions at the bottom of each page. The choices you make will change your outcome. After you finish your path, go back and read the others for new perspectives and more adventures.

YOU CHOOSE the path
you take through history.

CHAPTER 1

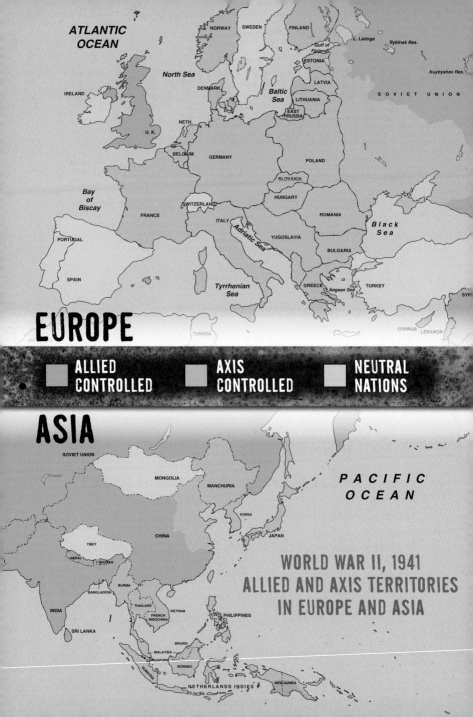

THE SECRET KEEPERS

You are living through World War II. It started in 1939. But the war's roots are deep, going back to the end of World War I in 1918.

The winning nations of World War I, including the United States, Great Britain, and France, forced the losers to pay a high price. For example, Germany had to give up some of its land and reduce its military.

7

During the 1920s Germans became increasingly angry at this treatment. A political leader named Adolf Hitler promised to make Germany powerful again. Hitler's Nazi Party came to power in 1933.

Turn the page.

Along with rebuilding the military, Hitler took away the rights of the country's Jewish people and sent them to concentration camps. He believed the Jews had weakened Germany.

Starting in 1936 Hitler sent troops into parts of Europe where Germans lived, claiming the land for his country. Meanwhile, Italian leader Benito Mussolini sent troops into North Africa. And in Asia, Japan was invading China. All three nations thought they had a right to rule other countries. These three nations became the Axis alliance.

In September 1939 German troops invaded Poland and then continued west across Europe. France and Great Britain joined forces to try to stop the Nazis. France, Britain, the United States, and other countries later became known as the Allies.

Agents from the U.S. Office of Strategic Services received Morse code training.

Some people secretly fought the Nazis in the nations Germany attacked. These resistance groups often received British aid. Even before the war, nations carried out espionage. Agents tried to gather information about other countries' military activities. Some of these spies belonged to special government departments, such as Great Britain's MI5 or Germany's Abwehr.

Turn the page.

Collecting intelligence—information obtained secretly—about the enemy became important once the war began. Spies also spread false information in order to fool enemies.

In the United States, military intelligence agents cracked the secret codes Japan used to send messages overseas. By the end of November 1941 President Franklin D. Roosevelt knew from these messages that Japan was preparing an attack. He knew the attack would be somewhere in the Pacific. But only on the day of the attack, December 7, did he learn that the target was the U.S. naval base at Pearl Harbor, Hawaii.

A stunned United States quickly declared war on Japan. Japan's close relations with Italy and Germany prompted those two countries to declare war on the United States.

Troops from many countries began to wage war in Asia and Europe. Fighting spread to Africa and across the world's oceans.

In June 1942 President Roosevelt created a new spy agency, the Office of Strategic Services (OSS). Its agents gathered intelligence, committed sabotage to stop enemy attacks, and spread false information.

You've always been interested in espionage, and you value the work that spies do. You also know that you risk being caught by the enemy. You might even be killed. But you're willing to take that risk.

- To be a member of the resistance in Denmark, turn to page 13.

- To be an agent working for Germany's Abwehr, turn to page 43.

- To be an American OSS agent, turn to page 69.

11

To reassure his people, Danish King Christian X rode his horse through the streets daily during the Nazi occupation of Denmark.

CHAPTER 2

RESISTING THE ENEMY

You are a college student living in Denmark's capital, Copenhagen, with your family. Since Germany invaded Poland, you've closely followed the events of the war. It's now April 1940, and you hate the Germans for their brutal ways. Denmark shares a border with Germany, so your homeland could be another Nazi target.

Early on the morning of April 9, you wake to a loud buzzing outside your house. German planes!

"We've been invaded," you say to your sister, Helena. "The Nazis are in control now." You learn they have invaded Norway too. The Netherlands and Belgium are taken next.

13

Turn the page.

The Germans let the Danish government stay in power. But Danish leaders have little control. And Denmark's military is too weak to put up a fight. You and your friends think that the Danish people can resist on their own. "We can start a secret newspaper," your friend Jorgen says.

You know that the official Danish papers can't print anything the Germans don't like. It would be good to tell people the truth. But you want to do more. "I've heard that the British are training agents to carry out resistance," you say. But Carl points out that you'd have to get to London first.

Maybe you should stay here to look out for your family. But you think you can do more to fight the Germans if you can get to London.

• To go to London, go to page 15.

• To stay in Copenhagen, turn to page 19.

That night you tell your parents about your plans to go to London. They're worried, but your father says, "I'm proud you want help defeat the Nazis."

Jorgen is going with you. You take a fishing boat to Sweden. That country has remained neutral during the war—they haven't taken a side. Resistance leaders there can help you get to London.

In London, Danes in the resistance direct you to the Special Operations Executive (SOE), a British agency. The SOE trains resistance fighters from all the countries occupied by Germany.

Turn the page.

SOE agents teach you and Jorgen how to be secret agents. You learn how to shoot, use explosives, pick locks, and parachute. You receive fake identity papers and learn how to disguise yourself.

After weeks of training, you're eager to use your new skills in Denmark. "We have two missions planned," a British officer says. "We need two men to parachute in with a radio so the resistance movement can easily contact us. If you go, you can take Jorgen with you. We also need one person to smuggle weapons to arm the resistance. Which would you prefer?"

You'd feel safer working with Jorgen. But just setting up a radio seems boring. Getting weapons to the resistance fighters would strike a blow to the Nazis right away.

• To help with the weapons, go to page 17.

• To go with Jorgen and the radio, turn to page 34.

You wish Jorgen luck before boarding a truck that takes you to an airfield. You board a British military plane heading to Lolland, a large island belonging to Denmark. The plane drops a huge crate of weapons. Your job is to follow and make sure the weapons get into the right hands. Your parachute floats you safely to the ground.

Husqvarna, a factory in Sweden, produced weapons and smuggled them to Danish resistance workers.

Turn the page.

Waiting for you is another Danish SOE agent. You know him only as Mr. Miller, which is not his real name. He calls you by a fake name too—Mr. Jensen. After speaking English for so long during your training, it's good to speak Danish again.

Miller tells you, "I have to take these weapons to a safe house and then give them to the resistance groups. You can come with me. But I also have a message for a resistance group in Copenhagen. You could deliver it for me."

You like the idea of going to Copenhagen. You miss your hometown. But you know the importance of building up the resistance in Lolland.

• To stay in Lolland, turn to page 36.

• To go to Copenhagen, turn to page 38.

"I'm staying here," you say. "Helena, you and your friends can help too."

In the weeks after the invasion, life is fairly calm. But Jorgen still wants to start an underground newspaper. You're tired of all the lies published in the official papers. You and the rest of the group find an old printing press. In Jorgen's basement you print articles that encourage Danes to resist the Germans.

Some of the news you print comes from the Germans themselves. Helena and her friends have become friendly with young German soldiers, hoping to learn secret information. Sometimes the soldiers try to impress the girls with stories about how they hunt down resistance members. And the girls learn the names of some German collaborators.

Turn the page.

You also write about the Churchill Club, a group of Danish teens named for British prime minister Winston Churchill. The teens carry out sabotage against the Germans.

"Look at them," Carl says one day to your group. "Those boys are younger than us, but they are really doing something to fight the Germans. We should too. We can get help from the SOE."

You know about the SOE. This agency based in London helps resistance groups across Europe.

Carl looks at you. "The paper's not enough. Let's make a real difference."

Sabotage is dangerous. But you fear what will happen if the Germans win the war. Maybe the Danes need to do more.

- To keep working on the newspaper, go to page 21.
- To join Carl in doing sabotage, turn to page 23.

"I'm sticking with the paper," you say.

In the months that follow, your underground paper prints more news about the war. Japan has bombed Pearl Harbor, and fighting is going on around the world. In 1943 sabotage increases in Denmark. The Germans say they will kill anyone who helps a saboteur.

All this time you've tried to stay focused on the war, but there have been troubles at home. Your father died after a long illness. Helena has delayed going to college so she can work. She and your mother want you to stay in school. But you feel you need to help the family earn money.

One day a man stops you on the street. He speaks with a German accent. "I know what you're doing," he says. "The newspaper."

Turn the page.

You ignore him, but he grabs your shoulder. "It would be a shame if something happened to you. What would your mother say?"

"What do you mean?" you ask. He explains that he works for the Gestapo, the German secret police.

"I could arrest you," he says. "But I won't—if you help me." He wants you to become a collaborator and tell him the names of everyone working for the underground newspapers.

"No!" you say. "Leave me alone."

"Think about your mother," he says. "Tell me what you know!"

You don't want to betray your friends. But your mother would be devastated if the Gestapo took you.

• To become a collaborator, turn to page 40.

• To refuse to help the Gestapo, turn to page 41.

"I'll join you, Carl," you say. Another student, Peter, wants to help too. You look at Helena. "Not a word about this to Mama and Papa!"

"Only if you let me help," she says.

"She can help scout our targets," Carl says.

Carl soon makes contact with a Danish SOE agent. He calls himself Markus. He uses a false name so none of you will know who he really is. You now have a small apartment of your own, and the group meets there with Markus. He pulls explosives and guns out of a bag.

"I'll teach you how to use these," Markus says.

Turn the page.

A mattress factory in Copenhagen burned after a sabotage attack by resistance members.

For several weeks you learn how to shoot a gun and safely plant bombs. Finally the time comes for the group to carry out its first missions. You've gained more members, enough to carry out two attacks on the same night. Carl asks for volunteers for each assignment.

"One target is the radio factory here in Copenhagen," he explains. "It's making parts for a German company. The other target is an auto parts factory in the town of Fredericia. Its products are now being used in German submarines. The radio factory has a few guards. The other factory is more heavily protected."

You like the idea of an easy target. After all, this is only your first mission. But the auto parts factory is more directly involved in helping Germany. Destroying it might hurt the Nazis more.

25

• To attack the radio factory, turn to page 26.

• To attack the auto parts factory, turn to page 27.

Six others join you in going to the radio factory. You split into two groups. Four men with guns stand outside the windows. You're part of the bomb squad. When your leader gives the signal, you and the other bomber smash the windows of the factory. "If anyone is in there, run!" you shout through the broken glass. You don't want to hurt any innocent Danes.

After a pause you throw a bomb through the window and then run. The bomb creates a fire that will quickly spread.

The next day word reaches Carl about the attack. "The bombs started a huge fire," he says. "No one will be working there for a while."

You smile, glad to know you've done your part to help the resistance.

THE END

To follow another path, turn to page 11.
To read the conclusion, turn to page 101.

You decide to go to the auto parts factory. The next day your group travels to Fredericia. Carl carries a suitcase filled with explosives and guns. When you reach the town, you visit a man who might have a job for you after you finish college. That way, you have an excuse for being in Fredericia if the police happen to stop you.

That evening you go to the factory with members of the local resistance. Carl splits you into two groups. You go with the men with guns. You'll protect the others who place the bombs. With your gun, you shoot a lock off a door. Inside are two unarmed guards. You see the phone is off the hook.

"Did you call the police?" Carl asks them.

"Y-yes," one guard admits nervously.

Turn the page.

"We need to get out of here!" you yell at Carl.

"No," Carl says. "Let's place as many bombs as we can and run for it."

The bomb group quickly sets the explosives around the factory and then lights the fuses. Within a minute you're sprinting down the street. But in the distance, you hear sirens and see several cars coming toward you.

"The Gestapo!" Carl says. "We'll have to run to the safe houses in town."

"But they don't know that we were at the factory," you say. "If we run, they'll know we're part of the resistance. If we stop, maybe we can convince them we just came looking for a job."

• To stop and talk to the Gestapo, go to page 29.

• To keep running, turn to page 32.

One car stops in front of you. Several men with guns get out. As the men approach, you see Peter is with them. He points at you and says, "That's them!"

"Peter!" you call. "What are you—"

Carl cuts you off. "Don't you see? He informed on us."

With Peter a collaborator, you realize you can't talk your way out of this. The Gestapo shove you and Carl into a car and drive you back to Copenhagen. They lock you up in the Shell House, which is Gestapo headquarters. You've heard how prisoners are tortured there.

When the Gestapo agents question you, you say you're a student looking for a job.

Turn the page.

"I don't believe you," the officer says. He punches you several times in the stomach. The air rushes out of you, and your ribs ache. He stops, but comes back every day, leaving your face bloodied. You almost say something so he'll stop the beatings. But you find the strength to remain silent and to protect your friends.

Your stay in the Shell House drags on. But one morning in March 1945, you hear the sound of planes. Suddenly a huge explosion rips through the building, followed quickly by another. Through a jagged hole in the ceiling, you see the planes are British! They must be attacking to destroy all the records the Gestapo has gathered on the resistance.

Then you see a fellow Dane at your door with the keys. "Come on," he says. "We're free!"

Danish citizens formed a resistance group called BOPA, a Danish abbreviation for Civil Partisans.

"What about Carl?" you ask.

He shakes his head quickly. "Dead. Let's go!"

You run for the stairs, amazed you're still alive, but thinking about Carl. As you flee the Shell House, you know you will tell his parents how he died so bravely fighting for the resistance.

THE END

To follow another path, turn to page 11.
To read the conclusion, turn to page 101.

"Let's go," you say. Carl follows you down a main street. You don't see any more cars, but you still feel scared.

"I think there's a safe house nearby," you say.

"Is it here?" Carl asks, pointing at an apartment building.

"I don't know." You knock at the door, but no one answers. Carl glances nervously behind you. "The Gestapo?" you ask.

"Run!"

You both start running for your lives. You don't look back, but you hear a car approaching. A second later there's a gunshot, and Carl stumbles.

"I'm hit!" he says.

"Try to keep running!" you yell as you pull out your gun and turn back to fire at the Gestapo. You realize you can't hit anything while you're moving.

"Duck behind that car ahead of us," you tell Carl. He falls to the road, blood streaming from his wound. Down on one knee, you shoot several times. One shot hits the driver, and he swerves. The car crashes into a building.

"Come on, Carl. We have to run." You bend down and try to lift Carl. "I'm not going without you." But suddenly you feel a hot stinging pain in your back, then another. You fall, dragging Carl down with you. You both die there in the street. At least you know that you did everything you could to protect your country.

THE END
To follow another path, turn to page 11.
To read the conclusion, turn to page 101.

Resistance fighters called their radio transmitter and receiver "the Phonebook," because it was the same size as the Danish phonebook.

The British give Jorgen a small radio he can use to send messages back to England. He'll use electronic signals to form words that are part of a secret code. To defend yourself, you receive a new kind of gun invented by the SOE. It's attached to a belt that you'll put on when you land. Your coat will cover the gun so no one can see it. You'll fire it by pulling a cable attached to the trigger.

That night you board a British bomber for the flight to Denmark. You don't say much to Jorgen—you're too nervous.

Finally you're over the landing target. A cord connected to your parachute is attached to the plane. When you jump, the cord will open the parachute at the right altitude. You look at Jorgen.

"Let's go!" he yells.

He jumps first, and you follow. You fall and wait for the chute to open. Jorgen's opens in a second. You panic. Why isn't yours opening? You twist around and see that the cord has broken off from the plane! There's no way for you to open your chute by yourself. You free-fall for several seconds, with the horrible understanding that your life will soon be over.

THE END
To follow another path, turn to page 11.
To read the conclusion, turn to page 101.

35

You take the crate to a large, beautiful house belonging to a woman named Monica Wichfeld. She greets you and invites you to stay with her.

During the next few weeks, you help Monica find more weapons dropped from British planes. One day Miller arrives with a man named Kieler. He's a saboteur, carrying out acts of sabotage for the war effort.

"The Germans are searching for him. We need to get him to Sweden," Miller says.

Monica says Kieler can stay there until they arrange a boat. After several days you lead Kieler through the woods to the boat. But near the water you see a German patrol waiting.

"What are you two doing here so late at night?" one soldier asks. "Let me see your papers."

You reach for the fake papers the SOE gave you back in London. "Where are yours?" the soldier asks Kieler.

Instead of answering, Kieler turns and runs. The soldiers fire at him. As they look away, you take out your gun and toss it in a bush. You would be dead for sure if the Germans found it on you.

The firing stops. You don't know if Kieler is dead or alive. The soldier nearest you pokes you with his gun. "Get in the truck."

They take you to the local Gestapo, Germany's toughest police force. You know what will happen next—you'll go to a concentration camp in Germany. You won't be much help to the resistance anymore. You only hope you'll survive the war.

THE END
To follow another path, turn to page 11.
To read the conclusion, turn to page 101.

"I can be most useful in Copenhagen," you say. "I'll deliver the message and help the resistance group there."

You arrive by train at night and meet up with Olsen, the group's leader. He explains their next mission—blowing up a mill outside Copenhagen. The mill is producing steel for the Germans.

On the day of the sabotage, you prepare a disguise. You don't want to take the chance of anyone recognizing you. You buy a bottle of the chemical hydrogen peroxide and brush it into your hair. Your brown hair slowly turns much lighter. You do the same thing to your eyebrows. You're a new man.

That night you go with Olsen and the others to the mill. But before you can do any damage, a spotlight shines on you.

"Halt!" A guard shouts.

You turn to run—you don't want to shoot another Dane, even if he is working for the Nazis. But the guard has no trouble firing at you. The shot misses, but now the German police, the Gestapo, are driving toward the steel mill. They fire at you from inside the car.

You fire back. Suddenly you feel a stabbing pain in your shoulder—you've been hit! You stumble as another bullet enters your chest. You fall to the ground, struggling to breathe. You look up and see a Gestapo agent standing above you. The last thing you see is his gun pointed at your head.

39

THE END
To follow another path, turn to page 11.
To read the conclusion, turn to page 101.

What will happen to your family if you don't do what he says? After a moment you nod. You confess everything you know. He tells you not to go to the paper the next day.

You walk home thinking about Jorgen and the others trying to help the resistance. You have betrayed them. You're now a collaborator. You'll stay alive to help your family, but at what cost?

Members of the resistance published *Free Denmark* and other illegal, "underground" newspapers.

THE END

To follow another path, turn to page 11.
To read the conclusion, turn to page 101.

The Abwehr quickly trains you. You learn how to operate a radio, which you'll use to send messages written in secret code. And you learn how to make bombs.

In June 1940 you board a German naval ship. From there you take a small boat to the coast of England. On the shore you begin to set up your radio, but you hear someone approaching. You pull out your gun and crouch behind the boat.

"Come out," a voice calls out. "We're armed."

It's local police, you think, or maybe the military. Should you do what they say, even though it would mean jail—or even death? Maybe you can blast your way out of trouble.

• To fight, go to page 45.

• To give up, turn to page 47.

CHAPTER 3

SPYING FOR THE OTHER SIDE

As war erupts in Europe, you are living in Berlin, the capital of Germany. Your father is British and your mother is German. You spent time in England as a child and speak excellent English. One day a member of the Abwehr comes to your house.

"We need people like you, who can pass as English. Do you think you can do it?" he says.

"You mean you want me to spy?" you ask. He nods.

You feel no strong ties to Great Britain or to your father, who left your family when you were a teenager. You are a German, and you will do your part to fight the war. You agree to become a spy.

43

Turn the page.

The swastika was the symbol of the Nazi party.

"I won't do it," you say. "Go ahead and arrest me."

"We will," the Gestapo agent says. "When we're ready. But until then we'll be watching you."

The man turns away, and you continue home. You look back in case he's following you. Maybe the Gestapo is already watching your house. They'll certainly watch you now, as the agent said. They must hope you'll lead them to Jorgen and the others, or maybe even more important resistance members.

You decide it's too risky to keep working on the paper. You know that you'll see Jorgen again, though. You just hope the Gestapo won't be watching you then.

THE END

To follow another path, turn to page 11.
To read the conclusion, turn to page 101.

It's a cloudy night, so you can't see clearly. You fumble in the boat, looking for some of your explosives.

"Hey, you!" another voice cries. "You speak English, don't you?"

You find a match and light it. As it sparks, one of the men fires. The bullet misses. You pull out your gun and begin firing wildly into the darkness. The men fire back, and several shots whizz close by. You realize that you're cornered.

"Stop!" you yell. You toss out your gun and raise your arms. As they come toward you, you see that they're police officers. They handcuff you.

"You're working for the Abwehr, eh?" one of them says. You don't respond.

45

Turn the page.

They push you into a truck and take you to a small jail. The next morning you hear planes overhead—German bombers are attacking England! Artillery fire at the planes, and you realize you're near a military base. Suddenly a bomb blast near the jail shakes the walls, and the roof crashes in.

As the dust clears, you see that the explosion has blown a hole in your cell. You could escape, but there must be soldiers nearby. Maybe you should just stay in the cell and hope for the best.

46

• To stay in the cell, turn to page 57.

• To run, turn to page 58.

"All right," you yell. "Don't shoot!"

You toss out your gun and walk forward with your hands up. Six men emerge from the darkness, each holding a rifle. You're glad you didn't try to fight!

The men handcuff you and put you on a truck. As you drive along you hear the men mention "MI5"—the British intelligence agency.

You soon arrive at a building. You're put into a cell. A few hours later five men come in. One of them sits down across from you.

"We want you to work for us against Germany," he says. "Let them think you made it here safely, and then we'll tell you what information to send them."

Turn the page.

"A double agent?" you ask. The man nods. "And if I say no?"

Another officer leans over and hands you some articles cut from local papers. "These men were German spies we caught," he says. "They refused to help." Each article describes the death of an Abwehr agent—by hanging.

You don't want to be hanged. But you're proud of Germany and all that Adolf Hitler has done to make the country strong again. Many Germans are dying for their country. Why should you be any different?

48

- To become a double agent, go to page 49.

- To refuse to become a double agent, turn to page 59.

You don't like the idea of betraying Germany, but you think of your mother. You can't bear the thought of her grieving your death. "All right," you say. "I'll do whatever you want."

An MI5 officer named Reynolds begins working with you. He gives you some money, but warns that you shouldn't do anything foolish. "We'll always have someone watching you," he says.

The next day Reynolds instructs you to contact the Abwehr. "Tell them you were injured when you came ashore. That's why it's taken you so long to radio them."

You tap out a series of short and long electrical signals called Morse code on the wireless radio. Soon you get a response: "Go ahead with original mission."

49

Turn the page.

The Abwehr used the Enigma machine to code and decode secret messages.

"What was the mission?" Reynolds asks.

"I was supposed to blow up a factory that makes warplanes," you say.

"Maybe you still will. Or at least the Germans will think you have."

Reynolds explains that the British sometimes fake acts of sabotage so the Germans will think their agents have finished their mission. That way the Abwehr won't know their agents had been caught and turned against their country.

The British begin a secret plan to trick the Germans. They put broken wood and metal debris around the factory so it looks like it has been bombed. Then an airplane takes a photo of the fake destruction. Soon newspapers are reporting the damage at the factory. You tell the Germans about your sabotage. Only the British government and you know it is all fake.

The Abwehr wants you to return to Germany for new assignments. A submarine will be waiting for you off the coast. But Reynolds wants you to stay and keep sending false information to the Germans.

You worry that if you stay, the Abwehr will get suspicious. But if you go back to Germany, there will be more secrets and lies to keep track of.

• To ask to go to the submarine, turn to page 52.

• To stay in England, turn to page 66.

51

"I think I should go," you say. "If I don't, the Abwehr might think I've turned. They might do something to harm my mother."

"We don't have to let you go," Reynolds says. "But I don't want the Abwehr catching on."

That night MI5 drops you off near where you're supposed to meet the submarine. The sub will send a sailor in a rubber raft to get you. You wait on the shore for hours, but no submarine shows up.

You set up your German radio and contact the Abwehr. A message soon comes back: "Change in plans. Go to Lisbon and meet Abwehr contact there."

Lisbon! Portugal has remained neutral during the war, so many intelligence agents meet in its capital city. You set up your British radio and contact Reynolds. He tells you to come back to London. The British will help you get to Lisbon.

You sit on the beach and stare at the water. You wanted to help Germany—and make money—but spying is dangerous work. If you don't go back to London, MI5 could track you down. Who knows what they will do to you if they think you can't be trusted?

Maybe you can convince the Germans to send you more money without Reynolds finding out. Then you can pay someone to take you somewhere to hide until the war ends.

• To go back to London, turn to page 54.

• To radio the Abwehr for more money, turn to page 61.

53

You radio Reynolds and ask him to help you get to London. Once there, you learn that MI5 still wants you to go to Lisbon.

Reynolds says, "Tell your German contact you're eager to carry out more sabotage. And perhaps he'll have new information he wants you to gather here." He explains that the British fear a German invasion. He's hoping the information the Abwehr wants you to collect could confirm that.

You take a British ship to Lisbon and meet your Abwehr contact, Leopold Wirtz. "I've heard of your excellent work in England," he says.

"We have more explosives for you, so you can carry out more sabotage," he says as he hands you a briefcase full of supplies. "Take this special pen too. It can be set to explode."

MI5 fooled the Germans with fake sabotage of the De Havilland aircraft factory in England.

Turn the page.

You nod and take the items.

"You're not growing tired of spying, are you?" Wirtz asks. "All the dangers?"

You're tired of everything—pretending to be someone you're not, owing your life to the British. You would walk away now if you could. But you can't say that. "It's all right," you say. "I chose it."

"Perhaps you should go back to Germany before going to London," Wirtz says. "The Abwehr could give you additional training in code-reading."

Maybe you could visit your mother in Germany. But Reynolds will be waiting for you in England.

• To return to London, turn to page 63.

• To go back to Germany, turn to page 64.

One of your guards is wounded, but he rises from the rubble and points his gun at you. "Stay right where you are," he says.

You hear more explosions and shooting outside the cell. The planes are still overhead. Through all the noise you hear something else—a loud whistle. You barely feel the explosion that destroys the jail and kills you and the guard instantly.

THE END
To follow another path, turn to page 11.
To read the conclusion, turn to page 101.

You crawl through the hole. Your guard must have been injured in the explosion, but you don't look back to find out. All around, you hear the sound of guns and bombs. You knew becoming a spy would be dangerous, but you never thought you'd be shot at so many times.

On the street you see an old motorcycle. At the same moment, you hear footsteps behind you. You jump on the motorcycle and desperately try to start it up. The engine sputters to life and you take off. But a British truck pulls out to block the road. You slam on the brakes to avoid crashing into it. British officers surround you. It looks like you're going back to jail.

58

THE END
To follow another path, turn to page 11.
To read the conclusion, turn to page 101.

"Kill me, then," you say. "I won't betray my country." After a quick trial, you're taken to Pentonville Prison in London.

Six German spies were hanged at Pentonville Prison during World War II.

In a few days you hear someone outside your cell door. You know the time has come. You feel tremendous fear as you think about dying. But you don't want to let the English know you're afraid. Let them see that a good German bravely faces death. A hangman leads you to the gallows. He places a white hood over your head and then puts a thick rope around your neck.

In a few seconds, a door beneath your feet swings opens and your body drops through. You die proudly, loyal to your country to the end.

60

THE END

To follow another path, turn to page 11.
To read the conclusion, turn to page 101.

You begin tapping out a new message to the Abwehr: "Can't get to Lisbon without money. Make arrangements to send."

The Abwehr agrees to send another agent by parachute to give you money. Someone will contact you tomorrow to tell you where and when to meet him.

Now you take out your British radio and radio Reynolds: "Will get back to London by tomorrow." You hope you can meet the German agent before MI5 gets suspicious.

You find a barn to sleep in and wait for morning. You hear noises during the night. You hide behind some hay. A few seconds later, a beam of light shines on the hay bale.

61

Turn the page.

"Having a good night's sleep?" a voice asks. It's Reynolds! You poke your head up. Reynolds and another agent stand there with guns.

"And I thought I could trust you," Reynolds says. He handcuffs you and drives you to London.

You're taken to a boat that ferries you to a small island off the coast of England. You're locked up in a prison with other captured German agents. You'll stay here for the rest of the war.

THE END

To follow another path, turn to page 11.
To read the conclusion, turn to page 101.

"I'd prefer to go back to London and carry out the sabotage," you say. "I can get more training later."

Wirtz gives you money and supplies, then makes arrangements for you to sail back to England. Waiting for the ship to leave, you think about all the dangers you've faced. Is this life worth it? With the money you have, you could live for awhile on your own. But where?

You go to the train station and look at the schedule. There's a train leaving for Madrid, the capital of Spain—a neutral country. You decide to go there. Maybe you can live a quiet life for the rest of the war—if the Abwehr or MI5 don't find you first.

63

THE END

To follow another path, turn to page 11.
To read the conclusion, turn to page 101.

Three versions of identity papers were created for the same man: the real paper, a blank version, and a fake.

"I'll go to Germany," you say. Just then a messenger comes in and hands Wirtz a note. He reads it, then looks at you.

"It seems MI5 has had good luck finding our agents."

"I wouldn't know," you say.

Wirtz holds up the paper. "That's not what this says. I'm calling the Gestapo."

You start to sweat. The Gestapo is a brutal secret police force. "The British turned me," you admit. "But I can still be useful to Germany. I can be a triple agent!"

"Too late. You're going back to Germany," Wirtz says.

You know what will happen there—torture. If you're lucky, the beatings won't kill you and you'll go to prison. In either case, your days as a spy are over.

THE END
To follow another path, turn to page 11.
To read the conclusion, turn to page 101.

"I'll stay here," you say. You radio the Abwehr telling them that you have more sabotage to carry out in London before you can come back to Germany.

The British have you send information about military activities to the Germans. All the information is true, but it arrives too late for the Germans to use. Still, they see you as a useful agent.

You sometimes send the Abwehr messages written in invisible ink. They taught you the formula that Germany created during World War I. You write the messages with a mixture of the chemical alum and garlic juice. When the Abwehr receives the messages, they heat the paper, and the ink appears. The Abwehr is pleased with your work.

In 1944 the Nazis believe the Allies will try to force German troops out of the countries they've invaded. The Abwehr wants to find out where the attack will come.

You send messages that the main invasion will come in northern France, at Calais. But this information is false. Your messages are part of an MI5 plan to fool the Germans. The real invasion comes June 6 about 200 miles to the south. The invasion is called Operation Overlord, also known as D-Day. Your false messages prevent the Germans from preparing for the attack.

In 1945 the Allies win the war, with your help, and you end your services for MI5. You become known as one of the best double agents of the war.

THE END
To follow another path, turn to page 11.
To read the conclusion, turn to page 101.

Jedburgh teams included agents from the United States, Britain, France, Holland, and Belgium.

CHAPTER 4

BEHIND ENEMY LINES

It's December 1943, and you've just completed training for the Office of Strategic Services. You're on your way to Europe for your first secret mission. You'll be part of what are called Jedburgh teams. You and other OSS agents will work with British agents from the Special Operations Executive. Joining you will be agents from France. You and the others in these special groups are called "Jeds."

Your training to become a Jed is intense. You learn how to parachute from planes and use all sorts of weapons. You're even trained to kill a man with your bare hands. You volunteered for this dangerous work behind enemy lines because you hate Adolf Hitler and his Nazis.

69

Turn the page.

Your family is Jewish. You know the Germans are rounding up the Jews in each country they invade. They send them to concentration camps. You think about the violent treatment and possibly even execution they'll face there. The sooner the war ends, the more Jews will be saved.

As you pack, your commanding officer comes in. "I know you want to fight the Germans," he says. "But I see that you studied engineering in school. The OSS could use you for some special work here in the States. Would you consider staying?"

You've trained hard to become a Jed and would like to go to Europe. But you know the OSS needs people in the United States too.

• To go to Europe, go to page 71.

• To stay in the United States, turn to page 84.

"I've trained too hard not to be a Jed," you tell the officer. "I want to go to Europe."

You and the other Jeds receive more training in England. You then wait for your first assignment in France, which the Germans have controlled since 1940.

On June 6, 1944, the Allies launch a massive invasion on France's northwest coast. Its official name is Operation Overlord, but everyone calls it D-Day. Their goal is to drive the Germans out of the country. The first Jedburgh teams soon land behind German lines. But weeks go by, and you're still waiting for your orders to go.

One day Major John Gordon comes to you. "I heard that you speak a little Greek," he says.

You nod. "My grandmother was from Greece."

Turn the page.

"We need volunteers for a special mission there." Gordon explains that the Germans may have developed a secret bomb. "The Germans can control this bomb by radio," he says. "We've heard they have one at a base in Greece. We want to find out if it's there."

The new mission interests you. It would be exciting to track down this bomb. But you'd also like to stay with your fellow Jeds.

• To go on the mission to Greece, go to page 73.

• To go into France, turn to page 78.

"My Greek is OK," you say. "I'd like to be part of that mission."

Soon you meet a few other men taking part in what the OSS calls the Simmons Project. You take a small boat into Greece. The Germans and Italians have controlled the country since 1941.

As you come ashore, you see a small German military boat at the dock. A sailor on board calls out to you in Greek, "What are you doing here?"

Angelos, another OSS agent, answers, "We're fishermen. But we didn't have any luck today."

You hear the sailors talking to each other in German. You put your hand on a knife strapped to your waist. If the Germans come aboard, you may have to use it.

Turn the page.

"All right, go on," the German sailor says.

You sigh with relief. Even though you're trained to kill someone with a knife, you'd rather not have to do it. But you know you'll come across more Germans in Greece. You have to be ready to fight.

The OSS thinks the bomb could be in several places. "There's an air base at Mikra. That's not far from here. Or you can take a boat and head for Athens," Angelos says.

You like the idea of staying on land for a while. But the base in Athens is bigger. It may be more likely that the bomb is there.

• To go to Mikra, go to page 75.

• To go to Athens, turn to page 85.

"I'll check out Mikra," you say.

A local resistance member named Spiro helps you get close to the air base. He lends you some sheep, and you pretend to be a shepherd. As the sheep graze, you scout near the base's main buildings. You see a few small planes, but nothing that seems like a secret bomb.

You send a message back to OSS officials: "No bomb here." The rest of your team can't find any signs of the bomb either. You feel as though you've failed, but the OSS knows not all missions turn out as planned.

Besides, the officials are already working on another mission. They want you to blow up rail lines that go through Greece. The Germans are using them to move supplies.

Turn the page.

A coded message instructs you to meet another agent. You'll know him by the large red ring he wears on his right hand. You go to your meeting spot. Several men walk by you. Finally a tall man slowly approaches. He scratches his left arm with his right hand—and there's the ring.

You know the agent only as Gus. He's going to help you recruit Greek guerrillas to destroy the bridge. You arrange for British planes to drop in weapons, and Gus talks to the local guerrilla leaders.

Soon the two of you are working with a small army of about 100 men. As you train the men, a messenger arrives. "The Germans are attacking a village nearby. They're killing women and children!" he says.

"We should go help them," a guerrilla says.

"Not in daylight," Gus says. "And they probably outnumber us. We have to focus on our mission."

The messenger looks at you. "Please help them!"

The SOE and the Greek resistance targeted the Asopos railway bridge in Greece to try to stop the German supply line.

• To help the villagers, turn to page 88.

• To stay and focus on the bridge, turn to page 91.

"I'd rather go to France," you say.

The night finally comes for your parachute drop into France. Going with you is a British officer, Rogers, and a French Jed named LeClaire. Your job is to meet up with the local resistance and arrange for airdrops of weapons. You strap your radio on your back. It runs on a battery and a small hand crank that also provides power. You also pack a rifle, your pistol, and extra batteries.

Before you board the plane, a British officer hands you a pill.

"What's it for?" you ask.

"It's an L-pill, in case you're captured. It's cyanide—it will kill you instantly. We don't want you telling the Germans anything important."

You wonder if you'll have the courage to take the pill if you need to. But if you don't, you know the Germans might torture you—and then kill you.

Another officer hands you a list of names. "These are the resistance members in the area where you're going. Memorize the names, then destroy the paper. We wouldn't want the Germans to find it."

A British bomber takes you to France. Your team members jump first. As you fall you see their parachutes open. Yours does too, but the wind has suddenly picked up. You drift into a large pit and land hard. The impact makes your pistol come loose and fire. The shot grazes your leg.

"Are you all right?" Rogers asks.

Turn the page.

"My gun went off," you say, gritting your teeth against the pain.

LeClaire talks to resistance members who have gathered to meet your team. They tell him there's a farmhouse nearby where resistance members are staying.

"Go there to get fixed up," Rogers says. "You can meet up with other Jeds later."

"The wound's not so bad," LeClaire says, looking at it. "We could put on a bandage and bring him with us."

The wound hurts, and it might be good to rest. But you don't want to miss your first mission.

• To go with your team, go to page 81.

• To stay at the farmhouse, turn to page 93.

"I'm fine," you say. "I'm going with you."

Luc, one of the resistance fighters, bandages your leg and you all walk—or limp—to a nearby barn to plan your first attack.

You get ready to send out a message on your radio. A resistance member named Emma enters the barn and tells you to stop. "The Germans are nearby," she says. "They have one of their vans." You know about the vans. They have special equipment inside that can detect your radio signal.

"Maybe a collaborator saw us land and told the Germans," Rogers says angrily. Collaborators secretly work against the resistance and aid the Axis.

Turn the page.

You look outside and see more German trucks arriving. Luc goes out to talk to the officers, pretending to be the farmer who owns the barn. Meanwhile, you and the others get your weapons ready. Suddenly you see the German officer shoot Luc! More soldiers climb out of their trucks.

You watch them creep toward the barn. You hold your gun, waiting to fire. Then one of the resistance men begins firing.

The Nazis developed a powerful machine gun, the MG42 (short for Maschinengewehr 42) in 1942.

"You idiot!" LeClaire yells in French. Soon the Germans are blasting their guns at the barn. Two of them set up a huge MG42 machine gun. It can fire 1,500 bullets per minute. Another sets up a light mortar, which fires explosives.

You aim for the mortar operator but miss. He fires the mortar, and a second later you feel the blast. It knocks you off your feet.

As the dust settles, you see that Rogers is dead and LeClaire is badly wounded. So are three of the other fighters. You realize that the Germans will soon storm the barn. You think about taking the L-pill the British officer gave you. It might be better to die now than to let the Germans capture you. But if they do take you, you could try to escape.

83

• To consider taking the L-pill, turn to page 96.

• To try to escape, turn to page 98.

"How can I help?" you ask.

"I want you to work in our research and development office. We've already come up with some great devices. We have a bomb that can sense when a train enters a tunnel and then explode."

You can see yourself working on new bombs for Jeds to use. You might design a weapon that could be used to kill thousands of enemy troops—more than you ever could as a Jed.

You agree to stay. Soon you're designing new kinds of explosives and guns. There's an explosive powder that can be baked into bread and a gun that's built into the handle of an umbrella. You're still doing important work to help the country—just not behind enemy lines.

THE END
To follow another path, turn to page 11.
To read the conclusion, turn to page 101.

Jeds used a variety of special equipment, including radio receivers, detonators, and small mines.

Alex, a member of the local resistance, ferries you to Athens. When you land at the harbor, you see a German truck approaching. Two soldiers get out and ask in Greek to see your papers. Your false papers say your name is Pavlos Popandreau and that you're a fisher from Volos, a town far from Athens.

Turn the page.

"Why are you so far from home?" one of the soldiers asks.

"I'm visiting a cousin here," you say in your best Greek.

The other soldier points his gun at Alex. "Come with us," he says. "Both of you."

You nod. "Just let me get my bag." In one swift move you reach for your knife and stab the soldier in the kidney, just as you were trained. He crumples and screams in pain. The other soldier shouts and raises his gun. You lunge at him, but you only stab his shoulder. You cry out to Alex, "Run!"

The German is too close to shoot you, so he swings his rifle at your head. It catches you in the cheek and sends you stumbling. Suddenly you feel something hot enter your back—a bullet. The first soldier you stabbed had enough strength to fire his gun. You fall forward and land on your face.

In a moment a boot kicks you in the side and then turns you over. You look up and see a German rifle. You know your first secret mission is also your last. You just hope Alex was able to escape.

THE END
To follow another path, turn to page 11.
To read the conclusion, turn to page 101.

Greek guerrillas fought against the German occupation of their country.

You turn to Gus. "We can't let the Germans kill those people," you say.

Gus looks at you and then at the messenger. "All right. Let's go," he says.

The messenger leads you and the guerrillas to the village. Even before you reach it, you hear the sound of German artillery. You look through binoculars and see the villagers running up a mountain, trying to get away. You lead the men closer to the village.

Hiding behind rocks, you order the guerrillas to fire. The Germans turn their guns on you. Good, you think—that will help more of the Greek villagers get away.

Your men don't have weapons that can match the Germans' big guns. But somehow none of the guerrillas are killed. After several minutes you order your men to fall back. You fire one last round from your Sten machine gun. Just then a small explosion to your left knocks you to the ground.

Turn the page

Looking up, you see German troops rushing toward you. You try to stand, but you fall down in pain. Your leg is broken. You fire your Sten at the approaching Germans, but quickly run out of bullets. In a few seconds they are standing above you, guns pointed.

You are about to become a prisoner of war. You will join the millions of Jews already sent to the camps. You had hoped to help save them, but now you will suffer just as they do.

90

THE END
To follow another path, turn to page 11.
To read the conclusion, turn to page 101.

You hate the thought of innocent people dying. That's why you came here in the first place—to save civilians. But you know Gus is right. Blowing up the bridge is more important.

Two nights later your group begins heading to the bridge. Only you and Gus know what your mission is. That way if one of the guerrillas is caught, he can't reveal anything to the Germans. When you reach the bridge you explain the plan. The guerrillas eagerly set up the explosives.

"We're almost done," Gus says. Then you hear the sound of machine gun fire. Germans nearby have spotted you.

Turn the page.

"Light the fuse!" you tell Gus. As he does, you and the others run. You sprint up the path, stumbling in the darkness and dodging the German bullets spraying around you. Then you hear a loud explosion. You look back and see the blast light up the sky. The bridge is gone. This mission has been a success. And you have a feeling there will be many more.

THE END

To follow another path, turn to page 11.
To read the conclusion, turn to page 101.

The pain is getting worse. "Take me to the farmhouse," you say. At the house the woman who lives there cleans and bandages your wound. Her husband brings a doctor to examine your leg. He says that the wound looks clean. You'll recover soon.

After a few days of rest, you make contact with the local resistance leader. He goes by the code name of Pierre. He takes you to the house where Rogers and LeClaire are staying with a large group of fighters.

"It's time for some sabotage," Rogers says, and the others nod.

That night you, Pierre, and another French fighter named Claude go to a local train station. You head to the stationmaster's building.

93

Turn the page.

Jedburghs planned and conducted sabotage and also helped local resistance forces fight the Germans.

"Is there a German train coming through here tonight?" you ask the stationmaster.

"I don't know," he replies. His voice and hands are shaking.

"He's lying," Claude says.

"You stay with him," you tell Claude.

You and Pierre go outside and tape explosives near a turn in the tracks. You also place a switch on one track to detonate the bombs. When the train's wheel hits the switch, the track will explode and throw the train off a hill.

But you can't stay to see your work, just in case some Germans survive the crash. You take the stationmaster with you as you head into the woods.

An hour later you hear a loud boom, then the sound of screeching metal. Everything worked as planned! You go back to your camp hoping that this is just your first of many successful missions.

95

THE END
To follow another path, turn to page 11.
To read the conclusion, turn to page 101.

Lying on the floor, you reach for the L-pill. You take it in your hand, which begins to shake. Can you do it? Can you really kill yourself?

You see one resistance fighter still desperately firing his gun, but he's severely wounded. Outside the Germans are still firing at the barn. You put the pill up to your mouth, then throw it to the floor. Nothing is worth taking your own life.

You get up with your gun in your hand. If you have to die or be captured, you should do it bravely. You remember all the people, Jews and others, suffering in the camps. You wait for the Germans to come in.

Second Lieutenant John K. Singlaub, part of a Jedburgh team, parachuted behind German lines in August 1944.

As the door swings open, you fire at two Germans, killing them. But three more storm in. Before you can shoot, they fire at you. At least you went down fighting.

THE END

To follow another path, turn to page 11.
To read the conclusion, turn to page 101.

As you stand up, you notice the back door. You call to the few resistance members who are still alive. In French you tell them your new plan.

"We'll give them one last round of gunfire, and I'll throw a grenade. Then we can go out that door."

Three men who are not badly injured agree. On your command they begin firing their guns. You pull the pin out of a grenade and toss it out the window toward the mortar. As the grenade explodes, you run for the back door.

Once outside you're relieved to see that the Germans have not surrounded the barn. You run as fast you can on your injured leg. The French fighters quickly pass you. You'll never escape on foot.

You see a briar patch in the woods. You dive into it to hide. Its thorns dig into your skin. You know it's a long shot that the Germans won't see you, but it's your only choice.

Fifteen minutes later you hear the Germans stop firing. You see them coming out the back door and into the woods. You try to hold your breath as they walk past you. They don't see you! After a few minutes the soldiers head back to their trucks. They're leaving—but not before setting the barn on fire. You lie there, scratched and in pain, but alive. You're determined to keep fighting the Germans until the end.

THE END

To follow another path, turn to page 11.
To read the conclusion, turn to page 101.

Hidden in plain sight: spies sometimes wore scarves that had code solutions printed on them.

CHAPTER 5

ESPIONAGE AT WAR

All the major nations that fought in World War II used espionage. At the same time, they also carried out counterespionage—they tried to stop the spying of their enemies. Some of the details of this wartime spying have only been made public during the last few years. Governments did not want to reveal all the intelligence they learned or how they learned it.

The need for secrecy and gathering information led to new methods of communicating. Special radios let soldiers in the field send messages over long distances. Invisible ink and secret codes made it hard for the enemy to read written messages.

The Americans came up with a unique way to communicate in the Pacific. Marines from the Navajo Nation created a secret code using words from their own language to send and receive messages. The Japanese couldn't understand the Navajo language and never broke the code.

Some countries did learn what their enemies were doing by breaking secret codes. Early in the war the Germans used a special machine called the Enigma to send messages. The British captured the machine and used it to learn when Abwehr agents would be arriving. This intelligence made it easier to capture the agents and turn them into double agents—or send them to prison if they wouldn't help.

Spy agencies also came up with new ways to kill their enemies or destroy property. Spies and secret agents used explosives that looked like ordinary items, such as a lump of coal. And at times they fought in hand-to-hand combat.

Jedburgh agents received weapons training at Milton Hall in Cambridgeshire, England.

Along with gathering intelligence, the sabotage work done by spy agencies and the people they trained played a key role during the war. Great Britain's Special Operations Executive sent agents to North Africa and Asia. The OSS also operated in those areas.

In the United States some OSS agents went on to earn fame in other areas. Julia Child worked in an OSS office before becoming a famous chef with her own TV show. Lawyer Arthur Goldberg volunteered for the Army in 1943. He ended up in the OSS and helped gather information about the Nazis in some of the countries they occupied. Goldberg later served on the U.S. Supreme Court.

MI5 still exists today in Great Britain. The United States shut down the OSS after the war officially ended in September 1945. But in 1947 the U.S. government created a new spy agency called the Central Intelligence Agency. Two of the men who later led the CIA also had served with the OSS.

Some of the secret fighting methods developed by the OSS are now used by Special Forces, highly trained groups of the U.S. military. Being able to learn an enemy's secrets and fight behind enemy lines is still an important part of warfare.

TIMELINE

1914—World War I starts.

1918—World War I ends; Germany is soon forced to give up most of its military.

1933—Adolf Hitler comes to power in Germany and begins sending political enemies to concentration camps.

1936—MI5 begins working with its first double agent.

1939—On September 1 German troops invade Poland, starting World War II.

1940—Germany invades Denmark and Norway in April.

In July the British government creates the Special Operations Executive to train resistance members in Europe.

Also in July German planes begin a major attack on Great Britain, known as the Battle of Britain.

1941—Germany and Italy take control of Greece.

On December 7 Japanese planes attack Pearl Harbor, Hawaii, bringing the United States into World War II.

1942—The OSS is formed in June.

1943—Germany tightens its control over Denmark as resistance increases.

Members of the OSS arrive in Great Britain in December to train to become members of Jedburgh teams.

1944—On June 6 the Allies come ashore in northern France to try to push German troops out of the country. The invasion is called D-Day.

1945—In March British planes bomb the Shell House, the Gestapo headquarters in Copenhagen.

World War II ends in Europe May 8, VE (Victory in Europe) Day.

On August 14 World War II ends in Asia.

Japan officially surrenders September 2.

The OSS is officially disbanded October 1.

1947—President Harry Truman signs a law that creates the CIA.

107

OTHER PATHS TO EXPLORE

In this book you've seen how the events of the past look different from three points of view. Perspectives on history are as varied as the people who lived it. Seeing history from many points of view is an important part of understanding it.

Here are ideas for other World War II points of view to explore:

- Some female agents worked for the OSS, helping get weapons to the resistance. What would it be like to have a dangerous job at a time when many women didn't work outside the home?

- "Frogmen" were excellent swimmers who were trained to plant bombs on enemy ships and blow up ports. They had special equipment that allowed them to breathe underwater, but they were lightly armed. The government told them there was a high risk they wouldn't come back from missions. Why would someone choose such dangerous work?

- The Danish resistance helped about 7,000 Danish Jews flee to Sweden when the Germans wanted to send them to concentration camps. The resistance used fishing boats, knowing that German ships patrolled the seas. Why might resistance members risk their lives to help the Jews escape?

READ MORE

Burgan, Michael. *Refusing to Crumble: The Danish Resistance in World War II*. Mankato, Minn.: Compass Point Books, 2010.

Gilbert, Adrian. *Secret Agents*. Richmond Hill, Ont.: Firefly Books, 2009.

Janeczko, Paul B. *The Dark Game: True Spy Stories*. Somerville, Mass.: Candlewick Press, 2010.

Senker, Cath. *Why Did World War II Happen?* New York: Gareth Stevens Publishing, 2011.

INTERNET SITES

Use FactHound to find Internet sites related to this book. All of the sites on FactHound have been researched by our staff.

Here's all you do:

Visit *www.facthound.com*

Type in this code: 9781429698986

GLOSSARY

artillery (ar-TI-luhr-ee)—cannons and other large guns used during battle

collaborator (kuh-LAB-uh-ray-tur)—person who secretly helps an enemy

concentration camp (kahn-suhn-TRAY-shuhn KAMP)—a prison camp where thousands of inmates are held under harsh conditions

double agent (DUH-buhl AY-juhnt)—a spy who works for one country's spy agency but is really loyal to another

espionage (ESS-pee-uh-nahzh)—the actions of a spy to gain sensitive national, political, or economic information

gallows (GAL-ohz)—a wooden frame that holds a rope used to hang criminals

guerrilla (guh-RIL-ah)—a member of a small group of fighters or soldiers

inform (in-FORM)—to tell police or government officials about someone's illegal activities

smuggle (SMUHG-uhl)—to bring something or someone into or out of a country illegally

underground (UHN-dur-grownd)—secret and done without government approval

BIBLIOGRAPHY

Beavan, Colin. *Operation Jedburgh: D-Day and America's First Shadow War*. New York: Viking, 2006.

Chambers, John Whiteclay II. *OSS Training in the National Parks and Service Abroad in World War II*. Washington, DC: U.S. National Park Service, 2008. www.nps.gov/history/history/online_books/oss/index.htm

How to Be a Spy: The World War II SOE Training Manual. 1 Oct. 2012. www.scribd.com/doc/46395261/33597374-the-WWII-SOE-Training-Manual-Rigden.

Irwin, Will. *The Jedburghs: The Secret History of the Allied Special Forces, France 1944*. New York: Public Affairs, 2005.

Kieler, Jorgen. *Resistance Fighter: A Personal History of the Danish Resistance Movement, 1940-1945*. Jerusalem: Gefen Publishing House, 2007.

Masterman, J.C. *The Double-Cross System in the War of 1939 to 1945*. New York: Ballantine Books, 1972.

Morris, Nigel. "*The Special Operations Executive 1940–1946*." 1 Oct. 2012. www.bbc.co.uk/history/worldwars/wwtwo/soe_01.shtml.

O'Donnell, Patrick K. *Operatives, Spies, and Saboteurs: The Unknown Story of WWII's OSS*. New York: Citadel Press, 2004.

Reilly, Rob. *The Sixth Floor: The Danish Resistance Movement and RAF Raid on Gestapo Headquarters, March 1945*. London: Cassell & Company, 2002.

Sutherland, Christine. *Monica: Hero of the Danish Resistance*. New York: Farrar, Strauss, Giroux, 1990.

INDEX

112